G000124390

Destined for Faith

Matthew Siddle

Onwards and Upwards Publishers

3 Radfords Turf, Cranbrook, Exeter,
EX5 7DX, United Kingdom.
www.onwardsandupwards.org

This first edition published in the United Kingdom by Onwards and Upwards Publishers (2017).

ISBN: 978-1-911086-48-2
Typeface: Sabon LT
Graphic design: LM Graphic Design

Printed in the United Kingdom.

About the Author

Matthew Siddle, a skilled foot-baller, found himself at the heart of the Hillsborough football disaster of April 1989. As a result of this traumatic experience, he began to suffer with a psychiatric delusion: that he was destined to play for Liverpool Football Club and give all his wages to the Hillsborough  Support Campaign. Now aged forty-five, Matthew Siddle has been in and out of psychiatric hospitals and mental health respite beds throughout his adult life.

Matthew worked as a journalist in the 1990s after taking a Postgraduate Degree in Newspaper Journalism at Sheffield College. He also later worked as a mental health support worker at the same hospital he'd been a patient at many times. However, his illness made it difficult to hold down a job for any length of time.

Bouts of unemployment and failed relationships knocked his confidence and he turned to alcohol. He lacked hope for the future and felt lost in the world. Then, on Easter Sunday in 2008, he had a dramatic 'Road to Damascus' experience. Jesus came into his life and opened his eyes to a truth he'd been running away from for so long. He dis-covered God's love and the chance of a brand new start.

Matthew's newfound faith helped in his recovery, ultimately leading to sharing his story through this book. The success of the Hillsborough families' Justice for the 96 campaign also inspired him to write about his experiences and encourage others who feel like giving up on life.

"Those who sow in tears will
reap with songs of joy."

Psalm 126:5 (NIV)

Destined for Faith

Contents

Author's Note

I wouldn't have been able to write my book without the amazing love and support of my family, friends and wonderful wife. Many health professionals have also given up their time to help me over the years.

I may never have recovered from the psychiatric condition I battled with for most of my adult life if people hadn't been so loving, kind and patient. They helped me face my fears head on and come out of the darkness into the light.

However, ultimately it was something else that reignited my flame and set me free, something so wonderful that I never saw it coming. You will find out what that was in the pages of this book!

I hope my story will inspire people to believe that a recovery from a serious mental illness is possible, and to see how that can be achieved.

Foreword by Anthony Clowes

FROM TIME TO TIME WE MEET people who have an immediate impact on our lives. The life stories of such people hold the potential to change the way in which we see the world. Matthew Siddle's faith story is such a story, both wonderful and remarkable in equal measure.

In 2008 Matt stepped from his local high street into a church building. That building was St. Luke's Methodist Church in the seaside town of Hoylake, where I was serving as Minister. Just three days previously Matt had experienced a great spiritual awakening in his flat whilst listening to an Easter gospel presentation on his radio and now, three days later, this radical conversion impelled him to seek out some fellow believers. Looking back, I'm convinced that God led Matt to our church. In the months and years that followed that day the impact that he would have on our congregation, and my own faith journey, was significant.

Matt is a passionate Liverpool FC fan. On Saturday, 15th April 1989, he arrived at the Hillsborough Stadium in Sheffield bursting with excitement at the prospect of witnessing his heroes progress to the cup final. What he and thousands of others witnessed that day would change their lives for ever. In the years after Hillsborough Matt's battle with mental illness would take him to the depths of utter despair. From a young man with the ambition and talent to become a journalist, Matt spent many years unable to fulfil his obvious potential. However, *Destined for Faith* is a very real story of a man who against all odds didn't give up and in time discovered a new sense of hope. If you, like Matt, have experienced the challenges of mental illness, I know that you will find great connection with the words that follow. If you are a follower of Jesus, Matt's story will serve as a great encouragement to you as you are reminded how God can take a broken person and begin a fantastic work of restoration.

I feel privileged to count Matt as my friend and I wholeheartedly commend his story to you.

Anthony Clowes
Lead Pastor, Potters Church
Stoke-On-Trent

Chapter One

Early Years and Football

MY EARLIEST MEMORY IS OF playing football on my own. As young as five or six years old, I recall kicking a ball against the wall at the end of my parents' and grandparents' roads. I could practise for hours without getting bored. I'd use a tennis ball to improve my close control and run around lampposts imagining I was beating defenders. Then I'd aim for the corners of the wall to try and beat the invisible goalkeeper. I remember doing a running commentary in my head pretending I was on 'Match of the Day'. I'd also play with my older brothers in the park. Often I would be put in goal as I was the youngest. This gave me a view of what the keeper sees when a striker is approaching him. I'm sure it helped later when the roles were reversed and I was the striker. I practised all the time and dared to dream of being a professional footballer.

I have a loving mum and dad and I am fortunate to be able to say I had a relatively happy childhood and some great friends. At an early age I realised I could run very quickly, which was handy when I needed to run away from my two older brothers. I won the final of the one hundred metres race at my junior school, which then gave me the confidence to outrun any defender on the football pitch.

I was moved up from a lower year at school to play for the senior team when I was only eight years old. Once I scored a hat trick in a big cup match, which got our school through to the final. During the main assembly the next day I was asked to stand up by the headmaster. I received a round of applause from the whole school for my goals. I was more proud of that than of any academic achievement or fancy certificate. It felt good being better than other boys at something and getting some respect for it too. I would carry that positive feeling into my teenage years. Football was becoming a very positive influence in my life. I was never happier than when I was kicking a ball on a football pitch, especially when I was scoring goals.

It wasn't just playing football but also watching my favourite team, Liverpool FC, which brought me great joy as a young lad. Being allowed to stay up and watch 'Match of the Day' on Saturday night was a real family treat. I was able to stay up late with Dad and my brothers and watch my favourite programme with the famous signature tune. Every time I watched the matches on television I couldn't wait for the day I'd be old enough to go to Liverpool's famous ground, Anfield, to watch my heroes in the flesh.

Finally, the day came when my dad took me to my first Liverpool match in the summer of 1981. I was excited for days before. The team at this time included some excellent players, such as Dalglish, Rush, Hansen and Souness. When the day finally came and Dad parked our car in the huge car park near Anfield Road, you could just make out the stadium through the trees, and there was an amazing buzz of excitement in the gathering crowd. A scarf and badge seller stood outside the car park on the way to the ground. Dad bought me a badge of my idol Kenny Dalglish and I proudly put it on my favourite red-and-white Liverpool scarf.

We went in at the Anfield Road end, which is at the opposite end of the ground to the famous Kop. This was it. I was about to see the Anfield pitch. As we walked up the dark steps that led to the terraces I wasn't disappointed. It was an amazing experience for a wide-eyed ten-year-old boy. We came out of the dark stairwell and had to shield our eyes from the warm sun to be able to see the immaculate hallowed turf. The green grass, marked out with its white lines, was in beautiful contrast to the clear blue sky. To me it looked like a glorious blank canvas. It stood empty, waiting for the players to tell the story and paint the perfect picture.

I was then hit by a sudden blanket of noise and colour. Red-and-white scarves and flags were all around us as everyone waited for our heroes to take to the pitch. We made our way through the supporters and Dad put me high up on the ventilation pipes right at the back of the stand. There I had an amazing panoramic view of the whole pitch.

I was so happy. All those years of waiting and finally I was here.

When the match started I asked Dad where the commentary was as I was so used to watching football on 'Match of the Day'. When I realised there wasn't any I was able to see the funny side of my question.

Liverpool played Tottenham Hotspur that day. The latter had Glen Hoddle and Ossie Ardiles playing for them but we won the match 7-0. The Kop was awe-inspiring that day – a sea of heads holding scarves aloft as they sang the famous anthem 'You'll Never Walk Alone'. I couldn't wait to be old enough to take my place on the Kop singing my heart out for the mighty Reds. At just ten years old my apprenticeship as a football fan had begun.

A few years later, at the age of thirteen, my dreams came true and I stood on the Kop for the first time. It was the European Cup and Liverpool were playing against Greek champions Panathinaikos. It was a good game to be at to feel the true force of the Kop for the very first time. European matches under the floodlights are always very special occasions. The atmosphere always seems to go up a notch as the Kop cheers on its heroes; Dad took me down to the front to avoid the crush of the crowd. I looked at the Anfield Road End opposite and remembered my first game, sitting on the ventilation pipes all those years ago. The Kop seemed ten times bigger and ten times as loud. Liverpool won 3-1 and our left back Jim Beglin scored one of the goals right in front of where I was standing. The Kop was like a monster that night, so loud and menacing. Even though it was exciting I must admit I remember being a bit scared too.

I had just passed my Eleven Plus exams and was now in my local grammar school. I was still playing competitive football and enjoying scoring goals, dreaming that recurring dream that one day I'd be scoring for Liverpool into the goal at the Kop end. However, at my school more emphasis was placed on academic achievement at this age, which meant that I could not put all my efforts into developing the football skills. Deep down, though, I perhaps also lacked confidence and the inner belief to seriously pursue my dream to play professionally.

My grammar school's sports were the classic middle-class combination of rugby, hockey and cricket. So they didn't have a football team, even though it is the nation's favourite sport. Instead I played for a very good amateur team called Heswall FC. We won a few trophies while I was in the team and I was one of their main strikers. Scoring a goal was an amazing feeling. Seeing the net of the goal bulge and hearing your teammates cheer behind you was a great sensation. Your goal rewarded the efforts of the entire team so everyone was happy with you, especially if you'd scored a really crucial goal in a critical game. It was one of the happiest times of my life. Football was without a doubt the main reason for building up my confidence as I always felt a bit out of my depth when it came to anything academic. Football gave me an identity and a real focus.

One of my friends at school was an Evertonian but I quickly forgave him when he got me a ticket for the FA Cup Final. It was between Liverpool and Everton at Wembley in 1986. It was the first ever Merseyside FA Cup Final, an amazing experience for a fourteen-year-old boy. It was also my first ever visit to the historic Wembley Stadium in London.

I had made a packed lunch for myself at 5am and I was the most excited I had been about anything in my life. This was the *FA Cup Final* and I was going to be there!

I remember the drive down the motorway. Supporters displayed the colours of the team they supported by putting scarves out of car windows and flags in their back windows. Some cars had red out of one side and blue the other. Merseyside had a chance to show the nation that we were united. It is a unique part of the country where families and friends can support either Liverpool or Everton but still get on. The comic banter over football has always brought the region together.

When we arrived at Wembley it was amazing. It seemed huge compared to Anfield. When I got into the ground I was sitting near the royal box with a side view of the game. I couldn't believe how lucky I was and I tried to savour every moment. I thought of my brothers as I knew they would be watching on television and cheering on the Reds, just like me.

The fans looked incredible at either end of the stadium, all blue at one end and red the other. Liverpool were losing 1-0 at half time to a lucky Gary Lineker goal. (Actually, it was quite a good goal but I'm biased, remember?) Then in the second half Liverpool turned it on and we won the game 3-1 with two Ian Rush goals and a Craig Johnstone tap-in.

This was Liverpool's first ever Double, which is when a team wins the League Championship and FA Cup in the same season. Kenny Dalglish was also the first ever player manager to win a Double. I was really happy for him as I admired him as a player, a person and a manager.

By this stage I was well and truly sold on being a football fan. I had also made friends at school with a group of lads who all supported Liverpool and loved going to stand on the Kop. These friends became my first drinking mates, in addition to my two older brothers who also enjoyed drinking socially; it was acceptable and fun.

A few of us went to the Kop every week as we bought season tickets. Liverpool had just bought John Barnes, Peter Beardsley and John Aldridge as we continued our domination of the English League. Part of the excitement of the Anfield experience for me and my first drinking mates was trying to get served in the local pubs outside Anfield before and after the match. Pubs seemed to me to be the most exciting places in the world.

CHAPTER TWO

Losing Hilary

AS WE WENT TO EVERY HOME MATCH we had made friends with a few girls who stood at the same barrier as us on the Kop each week. One of those girls was called Hilary. I got along really well with her, whilst intrigued that a girl could love Liverpool Football Club as much as I did.

Then tragedy struck. One evening Hilary was with some of the Liverpool players at a function at Anfield, then the next day she tragically fell off the back of a motorbike and died later in hospital. The story was on the front page of the Liverpool Echo and included a photograph of her with the article. I cut it out and put it in a frame in an attempt to keep her memory alive.

This was my first exposure to a real tragedy; a lovely girl dying at such a young age seemed so unfair and sad. Hilary had been just sixteen years old, the same age as me. I went with my friends who had known her to the funeral in a district of Liverpool. As you might expect, the congregation sang 'You'll Never Walk Alone' as part of the service. The song was now beginning to stir up all kinds of different emotions for me. There was even a wreath from Liverpool Football Club on the coffin that day bearing those emotive words in red and white.

The experience of Hilary's death drew my friends and me even closer to the club we loved and the next few games were all about her. Some of us even went to the Liverpool goalkeeper Bruce Grobbelaar's house, which was near where we lived. He had been one of the players who had met Hilary at Anfield the night before she died. We asked him to put a bunch of flowers in the net of the goal at the Kop end before the next home match as a tribute to her. Amazingly he agreed. That was an emotional moment; we found ourselves standing on the same barrier where Hilary used to stand on the Kop as Bruce put the flowers in the goal. We were with some of Hilary's best friends as the Kop gave their rendition of 'You'll Never Walk Alone' before the start of the match.

In the same week my grandmother arrived from Hull at my parents' house dying of cancer. She lived out her final weeks in our family home. The whole family rallied around to try and make her last days as comfortable as possible.

These two events led me to drink more alcohol than I should have. Drinking seemed to help me numb my pain and anger. It felt that I was being made to grow up too quickly, having to deal with funerals and witnessing death first-hand. Life weighed more heavily on me than it had before and drinking became a coping mechanism. The alcohol temporarily cheered me up and helped me block out the world. I was well aware of how it was altering my state of mind, but it seemed a welcome effect. Drinking heavily was already becoming a crutch and I was only in my mid-teens.

Exciting things always seemed to happen when I was out drinking. I was now getting served in certain pubs for the first time with a good friend of mine called Steve. We would wear suit jackets with jeans to make us look older and get a kick out of getting served as we were obviously under the legal age. We both loved the atmosphere in the pub and of course we loved the beer.

My football playing suffered around this time as I lost my focus and some of my fitness; I had started smoking as well as drinking. Teenage rebellion was kicking in as I was trying to make sense of the world.

Like me, Steve was a huge Liverpool fan and we started going to Liverpool away matches together. We followed our team, dressed in red, all around the country. It was good seeing new places and experiencing what other towns and cities looked like. We went to Arsenal, Chelsea, West Ham, Oldham, Coventry, Man Utd and Man City. Once we were halfway to Nottingham Forest when the coach broke down. We had to come home and missed the match. Fortunately, we didn't miss a great game as Liverpool lost 1-0 to a Stuart Pearce penalty.

Going to an away match was a real tribal experience. We were proudly representing our home city. In our eyes we were supporting the best team in the country who could beat anyone as long as we played well. There was always lots of singing on the coach while we watched old videos of Liverpool's past glories to get us all in the mood. On one occasion we sang Don Mclean's 'American Pie' as we approached Old Trafford, the home of our biggest rivals Manchester United. "Those good old boys, drinking whisky and rye, singing this will be the day that we die." I hoped it *wasn't* going to be the day we died as in those days an away match for a Liverpool fan at Old Trafford could be a bit tricky to say the least! We actually did get chased through the streets by about a hundred Man Utd fans after the match so not every away game was 'a walk in the park'. During this period, we also made several trips to Wembley Stadium as Liverpool reached a few League Cup Finals, an FA Cup Final and Charity Shield matches. Slowly I rediscovered some happiness after losing Hilary and my grandmother.

My own development in football began to get back on track. I was playing for a very good team called Bromborough Boys. It included some of my friends who were the best footballers from my school. We won a few trophies including the Cheshire Cup, which was one of the hardest to win. Despite the drinking and smoking, I was playing well, although no doubt I would have been fitter without them. Despite the distractions I was still scoring goals and still had a steely will to win.

I went on training runs along the beach to improve my fitness. The sand strengthened my calves and I would do short sprints in between lampposts when I was on the pavements. I knew I was fast but I wanted to be faster.

One of our players from Bromborough Boys was Graham Branch. He was picked up by scouts from Tranmere Rovers and had a successful career. He later played for Burnley FC too. A few of the players in that side could have made it as professionals; he was just the most dedicated and was also gifted with a sweet left foot, which is always an advantage. Despite not being picked by the scouts, I really enjoyed playing in that team. Maybe if I had been just a bit fitter and better focused I could have been given a chance. At that time,

I didn't really expect to be picked but with hindsight it would not have been impossible. We had a great side; everything about it was great. The training was fun and the banter between the lads was brilliant. The team had some talented players who created many opportunities for me. So I scored a good number of goals, which was a great feeling. I found some happiness, and playing football was the main reason once again.

Chapter Three

Hillsborough

THE EVENTS OF THIS CHAPTER would affect the course of my life for the next twenty years.

The tragedy happened on April 15th, 1989. It was the FA Cup Semi-Final at Sheffield Wednesday's ground, Hillsborough. We were playing Nottingham Forest. We had played exactly the same game at the same ground the previous year; Liverpool had won and the day had passed without incident. But this year was to be very different.

I pause at this point before I write anymore as it is very hard for me to think about and recount its terrible events. I am also wary to choose my words carefully so as not to offend or upset anyone. I stress that this is only *my account* of what I remember and it will obviously differ to anyone else's, even the accounts of my friends who were with me on the day.

It was a gloriously sunny spring day when the five of us set off from Merseyside. My friend's dad was driving his Land Cruiser, which we had used to go to away games before. There was a real sense of anticipation and excitement in the car as we couldn't wait to see our heroes get us into the FA Cup Final.

However, as we approached Sheffield on the motorway, we came across a hold-up in the traffic that threatened to make us late and maybe even miss the start of the match. Obviously we were not the only Liverpool fans in the jam and the mood in our car changed into one of worry and frustration. A nervous tension formed in my stomach. We couldn't miss such a big game, I thought. But just as we all started to believe we weren't going to get there the congestion subsided and we made our way into Sheffield.

After we'd found somewhere to park and walked towards the ground we arrived with only minutes to spare. To my horror the turnstiles through which we were supposed to enter were swamped with people. There was no sense of order at all. Policemen on horseback were desperately trying to break up the gathering crowd with no success.

I thought, "I'm never going to get in before the start of the match. We've come all this way and I may not even see the kick off. I might even miss an early goal, a Liverpool goal."

The sense of urgency to get into the ground was all down to timing. If the game had been pushed back half an hour, then the problem could have been solved. People were desperate not to miss any of the match. This meant some were being crushed against walls before the turnstiles while others were climbing to safety straight into the ground and side-tracking the turnstiles completely.

I was with my friend Steve and we were among those gasping for air as we were being crushed against a wall just before a turnstile. We moved inch by inch so we wouldn't lose each other. On reflection, the crush outside was in some ways nearly as bad as the eventual crush on the terraces. I was terrified of being pressed against the wall before the turnstile and I used all my strength to avoid it.

Thankfully we got through the turnstile unharmed. We didn't even have to show our tickets. The decision had been made by now to open the gates that led to the terraces. They were letting everyone in whether they had a ticket or not.

The real problems were now about to begin. We were shattered and sweating but ready to get into the crowd behind the goal. We really had no choice as the first thing you saw after going through the turnstile was a dark tunnel immediately ahead of you. In the distance you could just make out the green grass and red-and-white shirts of the players on the pitch. There was the same sense of urgency that there had been outside. Some people were even running down the tunnel so they didn't miss any more of the game.

When we got into the crowd Steve and I couldn't get very close to the middle as it was so packed. I noticed that both side sections of the terraces near the corner flags were virtually empty. Everyone seemed to be going into the terraces behind the goal. Within seconds I knew something wasn't right. I had been in lots of crowds before but this was different. There were eerie sound of cries and shouts of pain. People had started to panic and climb over the fence at the front and onto the pitch. I glanced to my right to see a man with a broken arm shrieking in agony. I was now painfully stuck on the edge of a barrier which was jamming into my hips and ribs. I too started to panic.

The match was now irrelevant. Apparently someone hit the bar for Liverpool but I wasn't interested. I had to get free of this barrier or I was going to pass out and get trampled on.

I suggested to Steve that we would try and get lifted over people's heads to the front and get over the fence. Thankfully for us, he had a better idea. He'd spotted a way out behind us. People were being lifted into the stand above. All we needed to do was get off the barrier.

At that moment the surge subsided and there was a brief opportunity to move off the barrier and get ourselves to the back of the terraces. As we did, we approached a large man standing against the back wall who was letting people climb up him. Others stretched down from above to lift you to safety. Climbing up would be pretty dangerous but worth the risk.

When we got to the top stand we could suddenly see the true nature of what had been really happening. Before I took it all in I noticed all the buttons had been ripped off my denim shirt in the crush and struggle for safety. As we stood looking down at the scene below, the players had long since left the pitch. There was now a sea of people rushing around. Fans were using advertising hoardings to carry bodies to the other end of the ground and there was one ambulance on the pitch. Then, near the goal, we noticed Dave's dad, who had driven us all to the game. He was walking there, looking at bodies, and suddenly the horrible realisation hit me that he was probably looking for us. I made a vain attempt to shout his name but he was never going to hear me.

I don't know how long we stood there for but it was soon time to go to our arranged meeting point outside the ground. We knew Dave's dad was okay but we were worried about our friends Phil and Dave, whom we had lost in the crush outside the turnstile.

It was a long wait but finally they turned up. We all hugged each other in turn. I think I was still in shock. The fact that any one of us could have just died hadn't registered yet.

On the walk back to the car, fans were telling each other the number of people who had died. The number continued to rise as we walked along. At first it was about thirty, then fifty, then seventy. It wasn't until we got home that we knew it was in the nineties.

The next day, I couldn't believe my eyes when my parents' daily paper was delivered. There on the front page was a huge photograph of a policeman carrying another one of my friends, Kev, unconscious in his arms. Kev had arrived early at Hillsborough for the game and had been positioned near the front. Now he was in a coma in a Liverpool hospital.

Kev was one of the lads who had gone with me to Hilary's funeral. A few of us went to visit him in the hospital in Liverpool. It was all too much for me. I fainted after seeing him; the sight of all the tubes in his throat got to me. Later I came around with my head resting on a nurse's knees as I lay on the floor. I felt both ashamed and embarrassed.

During the week after the tragedy I was one of those who visited Anfield to leave scarves on the Kop and fill half the pitch with flowers. I took the same scarf I'd put my badge of Kenny Dalglish on when I had gone to my first match with my dad nine years previously. As Kenny Dalglish was the manager at the time of Hillsborough I thought it was a fitting tribute. The net at the Kop end was also weighed down with scarves, and I found myself thinking back to the time Bruce Grobbelaar had put flowers in the same net for our friend Hilary. I tied mine onto the same barrier on the Kop where Hilary had used to stand with us on a Saturday.

A lot has been said about that day since and we have recently had the verdict of unlawful killing by the jury in the trial at Warrington. Finally, the truth has come to light and justice has been victorious; I feel so pleased for the families who lost someone. We all know a certain newspaper was a disgrace in the way it lied about the events of that day. There are still strong feelings on Merseyside against the paper and rightly so.

I have my own opinions about Hillsborough. All I know for sure is that it could so easily have been avoided. Firstly, there are the policemen who didn't recognize that the traffic jam outside Sheffield would mean a lot of fans would be arriving late. The overall management of fans at the turnstiles before the game was appalling. Necessary decisions were not made at the crucial times. Worst of all was the assumption that fans were to blame and the way that the police obviously closed ranks after the tragedy.

Immediately after Hillsborough I arrived home to Dad who had been watching the events unfold on television, not knowing if I was dead or alive. Dave's dad had phoned our parents from a shop outside Hillsborough, so by the time I arrived they already knew we were safe but there had been a worrying hour between the tragedy unfolding on television and receiving this welcome news. Dad hugged the breath out of me and I remember thinking it was a bit over the top. I must have still been in shock, not realising how close to death I had just come.

All those people who loved Liverpool Football Club had died just trying to watch a football match on a sunny spring day. It seemed impossible but it was tragically true. The fragility of life became starkly apparent to me and I believe my approach and attitude towards life changed after that day. After what had happened to Hilary and then at Hillsborough, I thought, "You may as well have as much fun as possible while you can."

The weeks went by and soon I was back in school trying to do my A-levels, with the exams looming. I was studying Government and Politics, History and English Language. The more History I heard the less it sunk in. I didn't see the relevance of 18th or 19th Century France. I realised I wasn't going to be able to carry on with it successfully with Hillsborough still on my mind. Mum and Dad agreed that I could drop History so I could try and concentrate on the other two subjects.

Slowly life returned to normal, and Steve and I would go out for drinks at the weekend with our other mates, Phil and Dave. For me, getting drunk seemed to mask the anguish about Hilary and Hillsborough. For a few hours on a Friday and Saturday night everything was forgotten. A new attitude was being born: live fast and play hard.

We never spoke of that day at Hillsborough. It was as if there was nothing to say. We knew it all anyway. That silence remained unbroken ever since.

My great hope is that all the families who lost someone that day will receive some comfort from the conclusions of the ongoing inquest in Warrington and that finally some kind of justice will grant them a measure of peace.

CHAPTER FOUR

Canada

ONE OF MY OLDER BROTHERS got married the year after Hillsborough and at the wedding reception an amazing opportunity came my way. His brother-in-law owned a hay-bailing business in Canada which exported hay to the top horseracing breeders around the world. I got in conversation with him and he invited me to come out to Toronto and spend three months working for him.

I didn't need to be asked twice. I thought it would be just what I needed after Hilary and Hillsborough. It was a chance of a lifetime that I was very grateful for. So off I went to Canada on the biggest adventure of my life, just eighteen years old.

My new relative met me at Toronto airport and drove me to his family home in a suburb of Toronto called Jane. His home was in a picturesque white-picket-fence district. It had beautiful green lawns and he had evidently done very well for himself. Little did I know, but I was to spend the majority of the next three months on my own in a motel room in the middle of nowhere instead of in the district with the beautiful white picket fences. I would spend the weekends in Toronto but the working week in the countryside near the hay barns doing the most challenging physical labour I had ever experienced.

There was a conveyer belt pushing three compressed bails into one for a man inside a huge container truck. He would then carry the heavy compressed bails and stack them one by one at the back of the huge container until it was full. The work inside the container was so hard the workers would share the time in there. The first time I went in I dropped the heavy compressed bail and landed flat on my back, much to my Canadian workmates' amusement.

One other incident that happened involved me and one of the huge container trucks. I'd forgotten to bring my lighter to work and wanted a cigarette. One of the guys gave me the keys to his truck so I could get a spark off the truck's lighter. As I started the engine, the driver had left the gears in reverse with the handbrake off. The huge container truck lurched back at speed straight into the steel doors of the farmer's barn, causing a massive dent. My heart dropped. It could have been the most expensive cigarette I'd ever had. Fortunately, the farmer was insured and everyone saw the funny side.

I was paid cash in hand at the end of every week. More often than not I would have no money left by the end of the weekend after spending it all in Toronto's many bars. I'd brought my attitude of 'work hard and play hard' across the Atlantic with me. I spent most of my time in an Irish bar called 'The Four Leaf Clover'. The locals seemed to take me under their wing as I was a young lad on my own from a different country. I played in darts games with the locals and got invited to parties after the pub closed, which was all great fun.

I don't know if it was because I was away from home for the first time but my drinking and partying went up yet another notch when I was over in Canada. Who's to say whether it was a reaction to Hilary and Hillsborough or just sheer teenage rebellion? This new attitude led me to trying cocaine at a party one night.

I took it at the studio flat of an ex-professional American footballer. The flat was amazing. It had huge wooden beams throughout and there were massive windows which overlooked Toronto's impressive docks. On that night there were beautiful clear skies and a full moon shining between the stars. The scene inspired me to put The Waterboys' song 'The Whole of the Moon' on the record player after I'd taken the cocaine.

Certain lyrics of the song[1] reminded me of Hillsborough, Liverpool Football Club and home. As I lay on a couch with a view of the moon through the window, the words ran through my mind and formed an unforgettably vivid impression. I was enjoying the feeling of the cocaine and alcohol but the lyrics made me feel uneasy; they seemed to be warning me against my hedonistic lifestyle.

The cocaine use was a one-off but it was indicative of my rebellious nature at that time. Although it felt good at the time, there would be horrendous repercussions to come.

My three months in Canada soon came to an end and it was time to say goodbye to the hay and the parties, and return

---

[1] You can read the lyrics online at
www.azlyrics.com/lyrics/waterboys/thewholeofthemoon.html

home to Merseyside. I was pleased to get back as I had missed my family and friends towards the end of my time away. That said, Toronto is a truly wonderful place and on balance I look back fondly at my experiences there. It was the first time I'd felt like a young man and not just a teenager. I was earning good money by doing very testing hard labour and then enjoying spending my wages at the weekend. It felt like I was growing up.

When I got home, a few of my friends had jobs working for the local council, so I too applied for a job at my local Housing Benefit Department. I wanted to earn money just as I had done in Canada. At that time a job seemed a much better idea than going into Further Education. I started date-stamping post, which was a bit mind-numbing, but after a while I was promoted to an assessment clerk so I was dealing with customers' claims and rebates.

There was a pub across the road called 'The Cleveland' which became my home every lunchtime. My friend Tony and I would play pool and have a few pints. Soon we found ourselves there *after* work as well. Life was fun. 'Work hard and play hard' was still my motto. I enjoyed drinking and spending a lot of time at the pub. I also began to discover spirits; until this point I had only drunk beer. Bacardi and Coke was the order of the day. There was a doubles bar in the pub so you could get a double Bacardi for the price of a single. It wasn't as if I needed any encouragement...

At this time, I shared a flat with my brother and I began to drift away from playing football. We lived for the weekends, when we would 'let our hair down' with our mates after a hard week at work. I'd brought that new party attitude back over the Atlantic with me. Monday mornings would be interesting, to say the least. Trying to get into work was like the plot of a 'Mission Impossible' film! Just twenty years old, I was still young enough to be able to drink heavily and recover in order to do it all again the next night. Soon I became quite a professional at it.

I made some vain attempts to play football for teams on occasion but my drinking and partying seemed to come first. I was carrying on what I had started in Canada, which was an unfortunate ability to drink more than anyone else. In alcohol I had found a dangerous new love.

In my defence I wasn't the only one with this lifestyle. I knew plenty of others around me who seemed to have something to forget through drinking and partying to the maximum. There was no shortage of friends who liked a drink in those days. It was socially acceptable. It was what brought us all together. Pubs and clubs were exciting places to be, where you could escape from all your worries.

My two brothers and I were like a comedy act in the local pubs in those days. We would compete for the floor, trying to make all our friends laugh by bouncing stories off one another. We were Big Sid, Middle Sid and Little Sid, and we really enjoyed each other's company.

We were all huge Laurel and Hardy fans as we used to watch them on BBC2 as we grew up as kids. We knew all the songs like 'The Blue Ridge Mountains of Virginia', 'Lazy Moon' and 'Honolulu Baby'. We would sing and dance with our mates inside and outside pubs, entertaining the crowds and ourselves. On my brother's 'stag do' we all went up to Ulverston in the Lake District, where Stan Laurel was born. There is a Laurel and Hardy museum there and they often hold conventions to celebrate landmark dates to do with the comic duo's history. Unwittingly, we arrived one week after one of these conventions, when the whole town had been swamped with fans dressed up like the pair. So, as you can imagine, when we too now all turned up dressed like Stan and Ollie it didn't go down very well. By the end of the night, when we all started coming out of the town's only nightclub, there were a few annoyed lads waiting for a fight.

We had all been dancing around and singing, which I don't think had gone down too well. A slapstick fight started and if you just stepped back from the fight for a minute it was a classic comical scene. There were seven or eight Laurels and Hardys in bowler hats and fake moustaches having a scuffle with four or five young local lads, just like in one of the classic slapstick black-and-white films. It wasn't a serious fight and it was over before it began but it will remain etched in my memory for a long time.

Things were good for me at this time. I felt that I belonged in this world of pubs, parties and laughs. Something was stirring within me though. When I was honest with myself I realised that I was escaping reality; the alcohol was giving me a false sense of confidence that wasn't there when I was sober.

I realised that real life and heavy drinking don't mix but I didn't learn the lesson. Instead I took my problems with me when I decided to leave my job and follow my dreams to become a student.

CHAPTER FIVE

University

IN PREVIOUS YEARS I HAD BEEN serving my drinking apprenticeship. That was before I entered the Premier League of drinking that was university.

I knew I needed a change and a chance to make new friends, so off I went with hopes of a brand new start. The housing benefit work had started to bore me and I needed another adventure like Canada. Perhaps I was just running away from responsibility again and trying to postpone the inevitability of growing up. Whatever my motives, I knew I was going to have a good time.

And so, just over a year since I had returned from Canada, I found I had itchy feet and decided to go to the University of Humberside. My grandparents and parents had lived in Hull. It was a city I had visited many times and felt I knew well. I chose to study Communication Processes, which was very much like a Media Studies degree. One of my brothers was a journalist and I had always been interested in the media and different kinds of communication. It also appealed to me as there were no exams; it was assessed by coursework during the year.

Both my brothers had gone to university and had told me what a great time you have. I didn't want to be the one who would miss out. Mum wasn't so sure though; she tried to persuade me to stay in my job at the Benefits Agency. In hindsight, her advice was wise.

My first two years at university were happy times. In my first year I lived in halls of residence and soon made some good friends with three lads – Terry, Will and Andy. We were like the four musketeers; we did everything together. During this year I just about got the balance right between a good social life and still getting the work done. I enjoyed writing essays and the challenge of researching for projects. We had a couple of inter-hall matches of football during the first year but I had lost my appetite for playing. If I had got into the university team, a different life may have opened up for me, but I did not take this opportunity.

I was very good at socialising by this point in my life, being a bit older than everyone else and somewhat more confident. After a few drinks I became really happy and something of a comedian. I was taking the first steps on the wrong path; I was doing too much too young.

My friendship with the other three musketeers had grown so much that we shared a house together in the second year. It was near our local pub 'The Mainbrace' on Beverley Road in Hull.

Many students would meet together in 'The Mainbrace' and this second year remains one of the happiest times of my life. My course at college was still going well, I had some great friends and I was having more success with girls as my drinking wasn't too out of control.

I was happy again. I didn't think much about Hilary or Hillsborough; I felt they were behind me. I didn't mention them to any of my friends at university as I felt it didn't matter anymore. I was starting to put the past behind me – or so I thought.

My third year arrived. I had been friends with a girl called Belinda in the halls of residence and in my final year we were still in touch. So when I was looking for a home for the coming year she invited me to live with her and two of her girlfriends. By this third year I had begun to lack focus. I had no real plan of what I would do after university. I was drifting and losing interest in my course after being in Hull for two years. It wasn't going to take much for me to have my head turned. The lads I had been sharing with in the second year had gone on placements so I had no option but to accept her offer. It was a big mistake.

We all shared a tiny flat and I had the smallest room, where you hardly had room to swing a cat. When I moved in I met an old friend called Jack outside the flat and asked him in. He lived just around the corner and he and his mates were soon coming around to our flat regularly. I think the draw of three girls was their motivation rather than that of seeing me.

Within a few weeks Jack produced some cannabis for us all to try. Instead of standing up and telling him I wasn't interested, I became the victim of peer pressure and smoked the drugs with everyone else. God knows why. I hated drugs. Alcohol was my 'drug of choice' and I liked the way it made me feel; it was familiar. Maybe I wanted to try something new or maybe I just wanted to fit in.

Jack continued to cast his spell and we were soon all heavy cannabis smokers. He wouldn't charge us any money, which unfortunately made smoking it much more appealing. I never paid a penny for all the drugs I smoked around that time.

After a while I soon found myself competing with Jack and his friends to see who could smoke the most, in the same way I had used to compete through my drinking. It soon became a competition in my mind to see who could out-crazy the others with their wild antics. I was sure I was going to win. I was beginning to spiral out of control.

I felt depressed by the whole situation but I didn't know how to get out. I stopped going to seminars and lectures and began to drink more than ever before. I was unhappy and the alcohol no longer cheered me up; in fact, it made me more miserable. I was a mess. Probably for the first time in my life, I didn't like who I was. I was ashamed of myself.

Then it happened. It was my twenty-fourth birthday. Normally it would have been a time to celebrate – but my world was crashing around me. I needed Belinda's friendship but I had been alienating people with my behaviour and heavy drinking. The cannabis, of course, was also still an issue. Jack was still giving us a supply as he was now dealing. Secretly I wished that he would just disappear or that I could make *myself* disappear somehow. I seemed unable to act. I felt totally trapped by the situation. I knew I'd let myself and my parents down as my degree was most certainly over. I hadn't been to college for months. I had been drinking every day for as long as I could remember and hardly eaten anything at all. I couldn't get through a day without a drink. I was losing grip on reality. I felt cornered, just like I had been at Hillsborough. I'd had no control then and I had none now. A nervous breakdown seemed just around the corner, but I had no idea how bad and how horrific it was going to be. There was nothing I could do about it. It felt like my fate. It felt like I was always destined to have a dramatic fall from grace. The last five years since Hillsborough had been building up to this.

It happened in the middle of the night. I was having a nightmare about having AIDS, which was the disease of my generation. When I was a teenager the television, papers and magazines were full of adverts with warnings about casual sex and the importance of using condoms. The dream had some standing in reality as I had slept around a bit over the years. When I awoke, the dream didn't stop; it continued into my waking life. I was convinced I had AIDS and was dying but had killed all the girls I had slept with too. There was only one way to save everyone. In my wild panic the only one answer was suicide. If I killed myself I would save everyone.

I picked up an empty pint glass on the side of my bed and smashed it into my face, hoping it would bring a stop to my horrible thoughts and spring me back into reality, but it didn't work. I had no idea how to kill myself. I ran down the stairs of the flat and into the street in a wild panic. It was the middle of the night and there was no one to be seen.

In the intense panic, somewhere in my mind I knew things would never be the same again. I'd gone past the point of no return. At that moment a plastic bag blew past my feet. I picked it up and tried to suffocate myself by putting it over my head. It didn't work but the wild panic thankfully subsided and I went back to bed totally exhausted and fell asleep.

When I woke up later that morning the delusion had not passed. All the girls had left the flat and I was alone. The panic returned and I needed help. Then the phone rang. I was in no fit state to talk to anyone but somehow I knew I needed to take the call.

It was Belinda. She said she'd heard me screaming in the night and had heard smashing glass. She asked me if I was okay. I couldn't even start to explain what was really going on in my head. So I lied. I told her I'd been drunk and fallen over on my face, landing on a smashed glass. She seemed to believe me as it sounded believable, fitting the pattern of my recent behaviour.

A minute after I'd hung up, the phone rang again. Again, at first I decided not to answer it, assuming it could be her again, but when I did it turned out to be a lifeline. The call was from my best friend Dave, whom I'd been at Hillsborough with. I managed to get the words out that I'd tried to kill myself in the night. He was great. He calmly told me to hang up and ring my mum and dad straight away and get them to bring me home.

I did what he said. That was the hardest phone call I've ever made in my life. I can't even remember if it was Dad or Mum I spoke to but they came for me immediately after I'd tried to explain. It takes three hours to get from Liverpool to Hull. It was the longest three hours of my life. I was petrified to leave the flat and didn't want anyone to see the scars on my face. I still believed I had AIDS and was going to die. My delusion was growing all the time. I now believed the whole world was ending and I was to blame. I was alone and slowly going out of my mind. Thankfully there was soon a knock on the door and I began to weep in relief. It was my brother. He had come with Mum and Dad who were parked around the corner.

It was a very strained drive back to Merseyside as my delusion only worsened. Eventually I was taken to Clatter-bridge Hospital, where I had been born. It was a place I was going to become very familiar with over the next twenty years.

I spent a few days at the hospital and recovered very quickly. On the day I was due to leave, it was beautiful outside. As I sat in the lounge of the ward, looking through the window, I saw a majestic double rainbow. At that moment I felt the closest to God I had ever felt in my life. I had a feeling of enlightenment. I was so grateful to have my sound mind back and be both sober and in control. However, I wasn't ready to let God into my heart. I didn't even know how.

The doctors and nurses suspected that the psychosis had been drug-induced and hoped it was just a one-off episode. However, this was not to be the last time. This episode of illness was unlike any other I had on later occasions but the thought of being responsible for the end of the world would always haunt me every time I subsequently became ill. I don't blame anyone for my drug-taking as I understand that ultimately it was my own decision; I could have said no. But I genuinely believe I wouldn't have smoked cannabis unless it had been brought into my life and offered to me for free.

I know now that I always had the potential to fall, that I was a time-bomb waiting to go off. At Hillsborough I was lucky; I found a way out. In Hull, I wasn't so lucky.

I hope this isolated story serves as a warning to anyone who is experimenting with cannabis and alcohol. Don't assume that it won't cause mental health problems, as it can and it does. I never thought I'd be the one who fell. I never thought it would happen to me. Like most young men, I thought I was invincible. I have met countless other people in psychiatric hospitals over the past twenty years who have become mentally ill because of cannabis, skunk, other drugs and alcohol. Don't let yourself be the next...

CHAPTER SIX

Mania

AFTER GOING ON HOLIDAY with Mum and Dad when I got out of hospital, I made another life-changing decision. I chose to go back to university to repeat my final year. The doctors thought my breakdown could have been an isolated incident and I wanted a chance to correct the mistakes I felt I'd made.

Unfortunately, after a few weeks of drinking on my return to Hull I had my very first full-blown manic episode. Hilary and Hillsborough were about to revisit my life again, if in fact they'd ever gone away. In a twist of fate, I had moved into the house next door to the one I had lived in during my second year, which was one of the happiest years of my life. Unfortunately, this time around was going to be a year to remember for all the wrong reasons. Maybe it was just being back in Hull; whatever the cause, I was soon losing my mind again. This time, though, it was very different.

I stopped eating properly and began to drink again as before. But instead of uplifting me, alcohol now had a depressing effect – and yet I didn't know how to stop. I felt under pressure to 'keep it together' but I was fully aware I wasn't succeeding. Once again I stopped going to college, spending more and more time in the student union bar and in the local pubs. In fact, it was in the union bar that I first had a panic attack.

I was standing at the bar waiting to get served. I knew the barmaid and she noticed I wasn't feeling well. I was short of breath and incredibly hot. She offered me a pint of water to drink but I poured it over my head instead, in panic. I thought I was going to die.

She helped me back into the cellar area where all the barrels of beer were. "I'll be back in a minute," she reassured me.

There I was, surrounded by alcohol and having a massive panic attack. I screamed out loud at the top of my voice in the midst of my panic and fear, and the scream seemed to echo all around the cellar. I was surrounded by the stench of alcohol and there were crates of vodka and whisky in and around the beer barrels. I thought to myself, "I've probably drunk all this and more since I was sixteen!" It was another inner warning that I didn't listen to, as I recognized the extent of my drinking.

These were the early stages of my illness; I was slowly losing control. I thought I was happy but inside I was crying out for help. I didn't realise it at the time but my obsession with football, Liverpool FC and my guilt over Hillsborough were now re-entering my life and tipping me over the edge.

I had a poster of Bill Shankly, the legendary Liverpool manager, in my bedroom and I had covered my walls with the front covers of old Liverpool programmes. I'd also plastered family photographs everywhere. Something had been stirring within me; I was looking for comfort that wasn't there, comfort from pictures of happy times, of people from the past and the present. I was so scared of feeling as I had in the flat all those months ago on my twenty-fourth birthday. I hadn't played football for a proper team since I was eighteen. I had been drinking heavily and I realised it had become a lifestyle that I was now trapped in.

Panic attack over and back at my student house, I lay on my bed looking at all my football posters, including the Bill Shankly one. Then suddenly a clear realization crossed my mind: I shouldn't be drinking; I should be playing football instead. It seemed so simple. I needed to put those football boots back on and start scoring goals again like I had in my childhood. "Who knows," I thought, "maybe I could have one last chance at being a professional." All I needed to do was to stop smoking and drinking, start to train hard, and maybe I could even be good enough to play for Liverpool. As I fantasised, my thoughts began to become delusional. Inside I was reaching out for anything that would soothe, and that something was football.

This is where it gets a bit strange but I will tell the story just as I remember it. I felt as though my body began to rise into the air until it reached the same height as my Bill Shankly poster. Then I seemed to hear him talking to me. I didn't believe in any sort of God so Bill Shankly was the closest thing to a God I had. I believed he wanted to use me to get justice for the ninety-six people who had died at Hillsborough. I believed he knew I had been at Hillsborough and wanted to put into practice his famous quote that, "Football isn't just a matter of life or death, it is more important than that." I was to be his voice, telling people what he actually meant. Like me, he was feeling guilty about Hillsborough, I thought.

Next I could hear the voice of my grandfather, who used to live in Hull before he died. He had been a very good footballer and had played semi-professionally. They both told me I needed to stop drinking and smoking and start playing football again. They promised to fix it for me so I would play for Liverpool. There was one condition though. When I 'made it' I must give all my wages to the Hillsborough Campaign.

I was 'on cloud nine'. I now had a plan to get me out of the mess I was in. I sensed great amounts of energy surging through my body and I felt invincible. I found myself feeling very close to a higher power – it felt as though God, if he existed, was guiding me. (Maybe I was only being guided to the safety of the nearest hospital!) My wrong conclusion was that God was giving me a mission to play for Liverpool. I felt that giving all my football wages to the Hillsborough Campaign was what He wanted me to do. I believed he had used Bill Shankly and my grandfather to get my attention. The whole idea didn't feel like it had come from me but from outside of me – from a higher power.

I jumped up, remembering there was a knockabout game on the university training pitches that night. And off I went, full of energy. When I arrived the game was just about to start. I knew some of the lads playing so I joined their team. Straight from the kick-off I got the ball, ran past four players and scored a goal.

In my mind I was untouchable now. Confidence was surging through my body. To my left I suddenly noticed the university first team training. "I should be with them," I thought. I started to dream up a way I could get fast-tracked into the side. Then I glanced to my right and noticed that, incredibly, Hull City FC had just finished training and there was the manager Terry Dolan. He was recognisable as his tracksuit had TD on it and I'd seen him on local television. I couldn't believe it – what an opportunity! "God is moving already," I thought.

I ran off the pitch straight towards him and confidently told him of my intention to become a professional. He said if I gave him the name of the team I played for and the time and place of the next game he'd send a scout to watch me. As I didn't have a team I was a bit flummoxed but not put off. I just reiterated that I was good enough to play for Hull City, as he and the rest of the players filed away.

That night I couldn't wait for the next day which would be a step closer to my aim to play football for Hull City. I went out, still on cloud nine, and in a local club I saw a girl from Portugal whom I'd met a few weeks before. She seemed to believe me when I told her about my plans to be a footballer. She wouldn't have known any better, I suppose. The previous week I'd taken her on a date to the new James Bond film and I'd taken a fake gun I'd bought in a toy shop as a joke. I'd worn a dinner jacket and bow tie, while she wore a red dress. I had clearly already been going a bit high.

The next day, after not much sleep, two events occurred that would send me spiralling. The first was that I noticed in the local paper that Hull City FC were playing Coventry City in the League Cup at Hull's home ground, Boothferry Park, that night. After meeting the Hull squad and manager the other day, I made the connection that I should go down to Hull City's home ground and see if I could get a trial. I was obsessed with the idea about becoming a professional and giving my wages to the Hillsborough Campaign for Justice.

Off I went, dressed in a tracksuit and with a gym bag over my shoulder with my boots in. When I arrived at the ground I knocked at the players' entrance. It was hours before the evening kick-off. When an old guy opened the door I confidently walked in and said, "Hi there," as I entered the ground. *I was in.* The old guy didn't suspect a thing. Maybe he thought I was one of the reserves.

I walked down a corridor and found the home dressing room. The gold-and-black Hull City shirts were all on their pegs. There was also a table with about twelve footballs on it. So I took a ball and ran down the tunnel onto the pitch. It felt amazing. Even though the terraces were empty it felt wonderful being on the pitch. I imagined what it would feel like with a full crowd and actually wearing the black-and-gold of Hull City. "My parents and grandparents would be so proud," I thought.

I made my way to one of the goals and started to take penalties. I aimed for the inside of the post so the ball would shoot around the back of the net. Then I tested my mission. I said to myself, "If I can hit the ball off the middle of the crossbar so that it rebounds straight back to my feet then I'm right in what I believe." So I smashed the ball as hard as I could. It wacked the middle of the crossbar and rebounded straight back to my right foot so I could control it in one. It all happened so fast. I was now in no doubt that I was right, that Bill Shankly was right, my grandad was right and God was right.

It wasn't long, though, before I heard a bloke shouting at me and striding across the pitch with some menace. It was

Hull City's groundsman. Despite my vain efforts to claim manager Terry Dolan wanted to meet me for a trial, he walked me to the exit and kicked me out. Even then I wasn't discouraged. I thought that Mr Dolan would hear about me being on the pitch and know it was the same lad who had wanted a trial the other day and then track me down.

I got home just in time to go and watch the biggest game of the season as a Liverpool fan. It was Manchester United versus Liverpool at Old Trafford. We had Robbie Fowler and Steve McManaman and they had the returning Eric Cantona; it was his first game back after his infamous kung fu kick at a fan when he was sent off against Crystal Palace.

To put it mildly, although I admired Cantona I didn't like him. I did something a bit foolish when I went to watch the game at the student union bar. I took the fake gun I'd taken to the James Bond film with my Portuguese girlfriend as I thought it would be funny to stand up in the union bar and pretend to shoot at Cantona every time he got the ball. Robbie Fowler scored two great goals in the game and Liverpool honestly deserved to win but we gave away a late penalty – and guess who scored... Yes, Cantona. Sadly, shooting my fake gun at him as he ran up to take the penalty didn't work.

As I walked home disappointed, I had my Liverpool scarf wrapped around my fake gun. If I saw a Man Utd fan I would point my gun and pretend to shoot them. I thought it would just be a bit of fun but I can see now that it was a sign of how I was slowly losing my judgement. Not realising what it must have looked like, I even walked into a shop to get a drink with the gun in my hand. The owner must have thought I was going to hold up his shop.

On the way home I decided to call in to see my Portuguese girlfriend. As I walked down her street I suddenly heard the screech of tyres behind me. There were shouts of, "Police, drop the weapon!"

I immediately threw away my fake gun shouting, "It's fake; it's fake!"

The police put me in their van and I explained the whole story. I told them about going to the James Bond film with my Portuguese girlfriend. I explained about taking the fake gun as a joke to the union bar to watch the match as well as my dislike of Eric Cantona and pretending to shoot at him as a prank whenever he got the ball. Surprisingly, they seemed to understand and after confiscating my gun they sent me on my way home without any charges.

One thing seemed certain to me. All these events indicated I was losing control. I knew it and so did all my friends. I was losing my battle to keep my dreams alive. I began drinking spirits into the early hours of every morning and keeping everyone I lived with awake by talking non-stop and playing loud music. I was manic and still believed Hull City would want me to play for them. I even thought they were going to send a gold-and-black car to pick me up from my student house.

Unknown to me, one of my friends had phoned Mum and Dad and they were on their way from Merseyside to try and get me admitted to the nearest psychiatric hospital as soon as possible. Those friends were very patient and caring with me and I will always be grateful they made that difficult call.

My parents arrived at my front door totally out of the blue. Then, instead of my gold-and-black car from Hull City arriving to take me to my dream of playing professional football, there was a police car waiting to take me to hospital. I was quite relaxed and playful about it all. I even asked the policewoman if I could wear her hat as I sat in the back seat. She agreed and so I sat with a police hat on, without a care in the world, still believing I was going to play for Hull and then Liverpool. I was sure I'd be able to persuade the doctors to let me go once they heard my story.

As the car pulled away I looked back to see Mum crying and being comforted by my friends. My mood quickly changed as the seriousness of the situation suddenly hit me. Suddenly my delusion took a dark twist. I was no longer destined to be a footballer; instead, when I got to the hospital I believed they would find out I had AIDS as soon as they took a blood test. I would be the enemy as it would prove I was the reason for the end of the world.

When they tried to keep me in the hospital I soon became aware that I had been sectioned under the Mental Health Act. I became increasingly frightened. The fear was so gripping that I got into a fight with half a dozen large men after I saw one of them had a needle. They soon pinned me down and injected me with some tranquillising drugs.

A few hours later I came around in a room with a few beds in but straightaway I saw a way out of the hospital, away back to playing for Hull City and then my beloved Liverpool Football Club; the doors to the bay room I was in were open and I could see another door just down the corridor that led to the outside lawns. Quickly I made my way towards the door, avoiding being noticed, and I was off. I was out of the door and sprinted as fast as I could to safety. I was a good runner, remember, and I was soon at the country road that ran alongside the hospital.

There was no sign of any traffic but after only a few moments a car came my way. I stuck my thumb out to hitch a ride. To my amazement, not only did the car stop to pick me up but it happened to be going past the very road my student house was on.

I still had a key for the house and I let myself in when I arrived. There was no one around so I went to find my best friend to ask him for a 'ciggie'. He was asleep and I think I must have given him the shock of his life when he saw my face as he would have expected me to be in hospital.

The injection I'd been given at hospital seemed to be still affecting me as all I wanted to do was sleep. So I took to my bed, back with my Bill Shankly poster, which quickly reminded me of my dreams of playing for Liverpool. I was back in the room where the delusion had been born, with walls full of photographs of family and friends; back at the place where I felt safe and loved.

Sure enough the police were soon called and I was dragged from my place of safety back to hospital, kicking and screaming after a struggle with what seemed to be at least ten policemen. They must have thought I was dangerous but I would never have hurt anyone. I was just scared senseless. The dark delusion had returned. When they arrived I was again convinced it meant I had AIDS and I felt I was being punished for causing the end of the world. As I was dragged from the house I grabbed my lucky Liverpool Ian Rush shirt that was on the stairs. It gave me some comfort at what felt like the most horrific moment in my life.

As I'd shown signs of violence I was taken to the high security unit, full of potentially dangerous and ill people like me. It felt like I'd been sentenced to prison for something I hadn't done. I was terrified but tried not to show it. Soon I was picked on by a group of three patients who were all from Hull. They had noticed my slight Liverpool accent so I was soon dubbed as 'Scouse' and identified as different. There I was bullied and threatened daily, mentally and physically. The threat of violence was always apparent and I had to have eyes in the back of my head.

It wasn't long before I found myself in a fight; not with the Hull lads but with a crazed patient who jumped around my neck from a window ledge, gouging and punching my head. It was totally unprovoked. Initially nobody came to my defence as I tried to shake him off. Finally, however, the nurses responded and prised him off me. They placed him in their version of a padded cell with a few mattresses propped against the walls. I instinctively knew I had to save face and that this was an opportunity to gain respect with the lads from Hull who thought I was an easy target. I told the nurses I wanted to make peace with the lad who had jumped around my neck and I was allowed in the cell to shake his hand. Instead I punched him as hard as I could in the face. It was the first person I had ever really punched and I didn't feel good about it. News, however, soon filtered back to the lads from Hull and I had the respect I needed for the rest of my stay on the ward.

I don't want to give the impression that all psychiatric units are like this. The majority are quieter places full of sedated and depressed patients. This was a unique experience. Out of over twenty admissions I have had, it was the only ward with so many violent patients. I must have been there for over two months. In that time, I eventually made friends with most of the patients, including the trio from Hull who had been bullying me. After a while there was a unity in our madness as we saw each other get better and change as people. The violence was just a cry for help, as it so often is.

During this admission I borrowed a suit from one of the other patients when I had an appeal tribunal. You had to go into a room which had three lay people sitting behind a desk. They would each ask you a series of questions and then assess if you were well enough to go home. It was the strangest interview I had ever have. In conclusion, they rejected my appeal and I had to serve the rest of my section.

When I was finally discharged I wasn't given any diagnosis or explanation for why I was so ill by the doctors. That would come later.

The whole experience served me well for the next twenty or so admissions to hospital and twenty to thirty visits to respite homes that were on my unwelcome horizon. It was the strangest kind of apprenticeship, a lesson in life that you wish you had never been taught. There was occasional humour but the biggest emotion was fear. After a few days you realise that the ward is your home and you try to make the best of a bad situation. By your eleventh or twelfth admission, knowing how the wards work becomes second nature. You know how to play by the rules. By that stage I was an old hand, or 'a lifer' as one familiar patient once called me.

At times, walking back through the doors of the hospital felt like coming home, it became so familiar. Often there would be the same staff and at times the same patients. The outside world became increasingly unfriendly and frightening after a few months of freedom. Trying to cope and rehabilitate proved more and more difficult as time went on. The madness of a psychiatric ward was strangely welcoming in comparison.

At least there were people who had the same illness as me and staff that tried to understand and help.

I began to develop a fear of freedom. 'Freedom' meant you started the period of time where you had to stay well to avoid another relapse and to try and not let anyone down. I knew there was never a guarantee that I wouldn't return to the wards. It was more a case of how long I would survive before I was ill again. I concluded that I might as well have as much fun as possible in the meantime.

CHAPTER SEVEN

Journalism

DESPITE MY TRAUMATIC EXPERIENCE in Hull I still obtained my degree. I completed it from home and was also given a special Endeavour Award by the university. For a while it meant nothing to me as I felt that I'd let everyone down and caused them avoidable suffering. But now, years later, I do feel proud of the work I completed and the award I received.

After university I was soon given the opportunity to work as a journalist. My friend Dave worked at a press agency in Liverpool and told me they were looking for someone to do some work experience there.

The most memorable times for me were going to the Press Box at Anfield to report on a few Liverpool matches. I rubbed shoulders with reporters from national newspapers like The Guardian and The Daily Mirror. But any respect I gained was soon lost when I would celebrate wildly at any Liverpool goal. On one occasion I interviewed Robbie Fowler about a play in Liverpool that had his name in the title. During the interview I was a bit cheeky and told him he had the best left foot in British football but I had the best right. Thankfully I had still retained my sense of humour! Of course, I couldn't forget the delusion I had had of playing for Liverpool. As a fan it was amazing meeting one of my heroes but I did find it a bit unsettling at the same time.

Some of the things the photographers and other reporters at the agency would do to get a story beggared belief. I had heard about the seedy side of journalism but you had to see with your own eyes to believe it. I soon became disillusioned and wanted out, especially as I wasn't being paid for the work I did. I frequented the pub opposite the office more and more often and soon my drinking was back to the level it had been at university. It served to block out my disapproval of what I was part of and what I felt I'd become.

After a while the inevitable happened. I had another episode of illness. If I'd wanted a way out this wasn't the way to go about it. In this episode my delusion was a little different. I believed I was destined to win the National Lottery and would become a multi-millionaire, only to give it all away to charity, most of it to the Hillsborough Campaign. The immediate danger of this delusion was that I started giving cheques to all kinds of people, including the builders working on my parents' house, in the belief that a large amount of money would be coming my way soon. I even wrote a cheque for a million pounds for my doctor as he assessed if I needed to be admitted to hospital. That was probably the easiest assessment he'd ever have to make.

While I was in hospital I found my debit card in my jeans and together with another patient we made a break for it and escaped for the day. We ended up in the pub opposite where I worked as a journalist in Liverpool. Foolishly I decided to confront my boss and tell him what I thought of journalism and his agency. As I clearly wasn't well I think he didn't hold it against me. Let's just say, when I was discharged from hospital a few months later I left the agency with his best wishes.

It was after this admission that I was finally given a proper diagnosis for my bouts of illness. On the day of my discharge my parents were called to a meeting with my psychiatrist and about ten other professionals in a big room at the hospital. I was told to wait outside with my parents until we were called in. Then, when we walked in, there were tables set out in a semicircle with the doctor and health professionals sitting behind them. In the middle of the room there was a solitary chair facing the circle, which was obviously meant for me. It felt like a scene from an interrogation.

The psychiatrist announced, "I'm sorry, Matthew, you have bipolar affective disorder, better known as manic depression. We feel you may also have post-traumatic disorder due to you being at Hillsborough."

I couldn't believe it. How did they want me to respond? I just stood up and walked out of the room in shock. I knew I was ill but I had hoped that it wasn't serious. Obviously, it was hard for my parents too and I felt so guilty to be putting them through it all.

One of the misconceptions of manic depression is that it is purely a chemical imbalance and 'all in the mind'. I believe it is triggered more by our emotions than anything else. We all have many different emotions like happiness, sadness, panic, excitement, love, anger, fear etc. My experiences have taught me that when you have bipolar affective disorder all those emotions can be so magnified that it becomes almost impossible to control them. The effort needed to contain them can often lead to sleep deprivation until inevitably you can no longer hide how you are feeling inside. Your mind just can't compute these extreme and very frightening emotions which can't be contained. In the end everyone around you, family and friends, will notice how differently you are behaving. This can't be easy for them at all as they will know that another episode is on the way.

The professionals also spoke about the possibility that I had a vulnerability to stress. They said that many of us are more susceptible to mental illness due to this factor. They talked about people having different stress thresholds, so due to the traumas in my teenage years I was more vulnerable at university when faced with further stressful situations.

Despite smaller bouts of illness and the sporadic drinking binges that followed, I tried to get back on track by playing football again. It was with a team called Wirral Athletic. I knew a few of the lads who played in the team. They knew I was a decent enough player and had asked me to join them. I was grateful as it gave me a focus when I really needed it.

I trained hard and got myself really fit. I ran on the beach again like I had when I was younger so that the sand would make the muscles in my legs stronger. At the end of my run there was a flight of about a hundred steps and I would sprint up them singing the theme to the film 'Rocky' in my head.

I loved playing football. As I crossed the white line the studs on my boots would touch the grass and transport me into a wonderland. Every game was like a beautiful piece of poetry and theatre. No match was the same as there were so many different outcomes possible. I was one of the strikers. If the game was at the other end of the pitch I would hover, waiting to pounce, on the halfway line. I would keep looking at the goal we were aiming at to keep a reference point in my head. I'd be checking where the keeper was standing in case I could lob him from a distance.

My brother also played in the team as a defender and we had a really good side. In one season we won the league and I won the Players' Player of the Year, Supporters' Player of the Year, most Man of the Match awards and Top Goal-Scorer awards. I was playing some of the best football I'd ever played and finding genuine happiness again.

There were often longer periods of good mental health during the football season. It gave me the weekly routine I needed and was something I knew I was good at. I took it seriously and wouldn't drink on the Saturday night before a match. I felt I belonged and was accepted by my teammates. This felt good, as dealing with my condition wasn't always easy. I hadn't played in a proper team since Bromborough Boys when I was seventeen years old and I'd missed it.

After two seasons, though, I felt it was time to move on. I had itchy feet again. I decided to go to Journalist College in Sheffield. Even now I don't know why, especially after my experiences at the press agency in Liverpool. Maybe I just wanted to avoid work and be a student again, as I didn't see myself holding down a proper job with my illness anyway. Despite everything, it was a happy time for me in Sheffield. My friend Dave had done the same course two years previously and had given me all his notes. The notes meant I had a head start when revising for my exams and as a result I qualified from college with no problems or stress. I soon applied for a job in North Yorkshire, not far from Hull.

So I was back on the East Coast working for a local newspaper called 'The Driffield Times'. Within a month there was to be yet another twist of fate affecting my future and my mental health. I arrived at work one day to find an invitation on my desk for an after-dinner event where Bruce Grobbelaar and Ron Yeats, the ex-Liverpool footballers, would be speaking. This was Driffield – in the middle of nowhere. What were Bruce Grobbelaar and Ron Yeats doing here?

I should have heard the alarm bells but I went along anyway and was granted an interview with Bruce Grobbelaar after the event. If you recall, he had been involved when Hilary had died. I asked him if he remembered putting the flowers in the goal for us. He did and was quite emotional about it. We ended up talking about Heysel (where thirty-nine Juventus fans had died before the 1985 European Cup Final against Liverpool) and Hillsborough. I forgot I was a journalist and just talked to him as one person to another. The situation, though, was stirring something within me. The old obsession of Liverpool that I was trying to leave behind was beginning to grow again. Suddenly, out of the blue, Bruce Grobbelaar gave me an exclusive story: he was going to apply to be the manager at Wolves Football Club.

I felt out of my depth with the information, not knowing what to do to sell the story. I felt totally inept. I made vain attempts to sell it to a national newspaper but with no joy at all. Then my drinking started again. I don't know if it was triggered by the conversation with Bruce Grobbelaar or by my sense of ineptitude at not being able to sell his story but I felt like I was losing control once again. It culminated in me missing three days from work and not ringing in. Things were not going well. I couldn't get out of bed and just wanted to hide from the world. The old fears were coming to the surface again.

I hadn't really accepted my condition at this stage. I didn't want to believe I had a mental illness and tried to do what everyone else I knew was doing. I was a young man but with a disability that I was ignoring. I confess that I didn't always take all my medication at the right time although, in my defence, it wasn't always easy to do so. I was still a bit of a rebel at heart and having bipolar is complicated. I couldn't always pick up on the early warning signs that I was becoming unwell.

Sure enough I 'got the sack' from the job and my mood continued to sink. I returned to Merseyside but it wasn't long until I was in hospital again. I was engulfed once more in the now familiar Liverpool delusion.

Without the knowledge of how to combat my illness I felt like a lame duck at times. I once described it as how you would put a chip pan fire out. You would make it so much worse by throwing cold water at it. It would explode into bigger flames. You needed to know what you were doing. Without knowledge I didn't have any power over my condition. Yes, stresses around the time I was ill didn't help but in the end I believe I was a ticking time bomb waiting to go off.

It is possible that I was on the verge of being ill for many years before I actually had a manic episode. I was always a bit wilder and a bit more rebellious than anyone else. I seemed to view the world in a different way to my brothers, friends and peers. I didn't want to conform or play by the rules. I couldn't understand why everyone wanted a job or a wife and kids. I liked to question everything.

In this current state of life, women were a problem for me. Whenever I met someone I liked, I was invariably over-confident. I would fall for women far too easily. Being close to someone would often be dangerous and normally push me way over the edge, push me back to hospital. There were a number of failed romances that only lasted about a week or two. They could have gone somewhere if it wasn't for my illness. This obviously left me jaded and bitter, not to mention heartbroken. It put me off trying to find romance. Was I ever going to fall in love and sustain it with this illness, or was I destined to be single for ever? Every time I got close to love I would end up in hospital and never see the girl again. It was a tough time and I often felt like giving up.

I tried to focus on playing football again for a team in Birkenhead called 'The Victoria Lodge'. At one of our training sessions Jason McAteer came along. He knew our manager and was on Bolton Wanderers' books at the time. He was later to sign for Liverpool. His first touch was amazing and he was very fit; you could see why he became such a good player.

This attempt at playing wasn't as successful as before. I was no longer as fit as I had been and I felt like a bit of an outsider in the squad. The whole experience left me feeling depressed. Up to this point, football had always made me happy, but now I found that crossing the white line was more like a nightmare than a wonderland and my boots seemed to stick to the grass like glue. Not being able to establish myself in the side, I left after only one season. Soon I was back in hospital again, not with a mania but with a more depressive episode.

During my stay at hospital, a lad on the wards who was going to an Alcoholics Anonymous meeting asked me if I would go with him for moral support. I agreed, and during the meeting I heard all the stories of why people drank. As I recognised their feelings and their desire to get drunk, I began to suspect that I too might have a drinking problem. As I thought it through further, I concluded that alcohol could be to blame for all my problems going right back to my teenage years. I suspected I might even be an alcoholic. When I was discharged from hospital, I continued to go to the AA meetings – about ten of them. However, doubts began to enter my mind as to whether I really had the same serious, life-changing problems as some of the people I was meeting. Was I really an addict?

In fact, I did have a problem with alcohol but was not a full-blown addict. I drank too much but I didn't have the complete dependency and compulsion I was hearing about in the meetings. I didn't want to give up on an 'old friend' that made me happy and helped me to relax. I was unwilling to let go – to let go of my old life and be truly free. I was still afraid of my own freedom.

CHAPTER EIGHT

Rosewarne and Supported Living

OVER THE YEARS I HAD STARTED going to a respite home on the Wirral called Rosewarne. It was a lovely old Tudor building with nice gardens in a good area. The facility was designed to help people avoid admission to hospital when the early signs of an episode became visible. It also offered respite to mental health patients in the community who needed a few days' rest. There were about ten bedrooms, a twenty-four-hour staff rota and even a chef to provide food during your stay.

I used Rosewarne at various stages of illness and stayed on many occasions. Sometimes I was very ill and it was just a matter of time before I was taken to hospital; on other occasions the stay served to alleviate the panic of believing I was becoming ill. It was a safe haven, a place to try and relax away from the stresses of the outside world.

After a few years you started to notice the same people were coming and going and it became like a community of its own. There was the same unity you would find in hospital.

The patients would often help each other as they knew exactly what it was like to suffer with a mental health condition.

One of the first times I went there I was in the middle of a manic episode. I was totally convinced I was going to play for Liverpool and give my wages to the Hillsborough Campaign once again. My doctor was due to arrive to assess whether I needed to go to hospital while the staff were trying to keep me in the building. As it was a gorgeous, sunny day I wanted to be outside and managed to get out. I walked onto the pavement on the corner of the main street where there was a big, old-fashioned red letter box.

As I was consumed with Liverpool Football Club I decided to sing to the whole street. I climbed on top of the post box and started singing 'You'll Never Walk Alone' at the top of my voice. It was a song I associated with some of the saddest parts of my teenage years, as well as some of the happiest when I used to sing it in joy on the Kop. It had now become a bittersweet anthem. I was in the middle of the third verse when who drove past the letter box but my doctor. I think my public display was enough to sway his decision on whether to admit me to hospital.

Humour aside, staying at Rosewarne could be very hard work. You had to cope with being mentally ill as well as accommodating everyone else in the building. Like in hospital, finding a friend was the key. So you hoped and prayed that someone you knew would be there to make your stay go well.

In 2000 I was to move into supported living accommodation in an attempt to stabilise my illness and prevent the frequency of my episodes and admissions to Rosewarne and hospital. Previously I had been living in a shared house with three other people for four years. My friend Dave part-owned the house and was one of the people living there. It was an exciting time as we all got on well and went out drinking together. It felt a bit like my student days again. However, I needed some stability as I had been ill a lot while there.

Often, when the anniversary of Hillsborough came around on 15th April, I would relapse and have to be admitted to hospital. Every Liverpool match in that week would have a minute's silence and the local papers would have tributes to the ninety-six who died. The memories would flood back, not only of the day itself but of times I'd been ill before. It often brought out the worst in me as I would get bitter and angry about my own situation. Some years I'd be so busy having fun with my friends that I would forget what day it was and feel very guilty when I realised the date.

There was something else that happened, and still happens today. At crucial times throughout my life I would glance at the clock and it would be 3.06pm, the time the match was stopped at Hillsborough. Obviously I found this really upsetting and I'm sure other survivors and families of those whose loved ones didn't come home have also had this happen to them since 15th April, 1989.

The shared house had changed a lot and the memories of Hillsborough I had there had swayed my decision to leave. A few of my best friends had recently moved on so I felt the need for a change. But I didn't know anyone else to share with. So I decided to try shared living accommodation, which wasn't really ideal but I was running out of options. I thought it would only be a stop gap but I didn't know I would spend the next seven years of my life there and nearly lose myself completely in the process. I was living with other people suffering from mental health conditions who were often using alcohol and drugs to cope. This was hard for me when I was trying to stay sober and stay well.

The place I moved into was truly amazing. It was an old converted coach house with a beautiful stone exterior and wooden beams throughout. Despite the issues with the other residents I would have been a fool to turn down the chance of living there. At the beginning I thought I was very lucky. The house was in an exclusive area and was set back from the road with beautiful front and back gardens. I had no plan for my own future at this point as I was still being ruled by my illness. I felt weak and tired. I'd been battered around for so long by my condition. Life seemed unfair and I just needed a place to try and get strong again.

I was twenty-nine when I moved in and would be approaching my late thirties by the time I moved out – which was not in the plan, if I had any plan at all. Your thirties are when you would normally be establishing yourself in your career, a time for getting married and having a family, but I was lost in what felt more like the Bermuda Triangle. I've talked earlier about apprenticeships. This was definitely another apprenticeship for life that you couldn't possibly understand unless you lived there. It could very easily have broken me but many people played their part in helping me and showing me the way out of my personal prison and pain.

I lost my hope in those seven years. Every door seemed to close in front of me like a cruel maze. The house was like a web and I felt like the fly. Support staff came in once a day to check we were all okay. I knew they were only doing their job but for years I just craved my own space – somewhere I could call my own, somewhere I could find my own peace. It seemed an impossible dream as I felt I had no strength to improve my life. Ultimately, though, I was paralyzed by my fear of freedom; I was stuck in a rut, unable and often unwilling to act. I lived in supported living with a severe mental illness, with no job and no prospects. The future looked bleak. These were the lost years, a time where everything seemed to stand still.

Throughout this period Mum and Dad were amazing. Their love kept me hanging on in there by my fingernails, so much so that in 2004 Mum asked me if I wanted to join her on a committee for a new mental health team called Early Intervention Into Psychosis. Mum was heavily involved in championing improvements for mental health for carers and service users. She went to lots of meetings and committees and was a respected contributor, a role she continued to have for many years. At first I was reluctant but I liked the idea of supporting young people with the early signs of psychosis and thought I had something to offer with my past experiences.

In 2005 I reached the milestone of staying well for six months – quite an achievement at this stage of my recovery. I had been sitting on the NHS Committee for the Early Intervention Into Psychosis team for five of those months. I was their Service User Representative, giving advice from someone who had experience of having psychosis and being on psychiatric wards.

When I heard a team was being set up near where I lived I became interested in the possibility of joining the workforce again. I saw it as an opportunity of getting out of my supported living house, getting my own flat and finally moving on. I applied for the job as a support worker and was successful.

When I started the job the office was not in an independent building away from the hospital as I'd been told but on an old ward at the same psychiatric unit where I'd been a patient so many times before. As it was the same hospital, all the bad memories came flooding back. Already on the first day working there I found myself asking why I had thought this job would be a good idea. In the days to come it felt like torture every time I arrived at the hospital doors. It was a real test of my character and my courage.

Throughout this tremendously difficult time, I felt God at my side. I would often visit the hospital chapel before going into work and ask him to help me. I had something of a love/hate relationship with God at this time. Part of me felt angry at him for all the suffering I'd been put through, yet at the same time, I was willing to try and communicate through prayer as it did offer me some peace and comfort.

In my job I was dealing with young people who had the early signs of psychosis and I helped assess them in the community and on the wards. I regularly went onto the same ward where I'd been a patient as recently as six months before. I felt totally out of my depth. I knew most of the nurses and patients, and I could see they were confused that I was now a member of staff. I was also working alongside health professionals with years of experience. I was worried they didn't think I had the proper credentials for the role. After four months I knew I had to leave but how could I tell my parents who were so excited by how well I was doing and the progress I had made?

The way I got out was the worst imaginable. I was still living in supported living accommodation with two lads who were drinking heavily and occasionally smoking cannabis.

Unfortunately, on one of the nights they were taking the drug I was very drunk and vulnerable to having one night of escapism. Even after my past experiences with cannabis I thought, "Surely it can't happen again; surely smoking this won't make me ill." But sadly for me, and for my friends and family, it did.

I was thirty-three but within a few days I was again convinced I was going to play for Liverpool and give all my wages to the Hillsborough Campaign. The fact that the delusion kept coming back over the years just seemed to confirm to me that it must be true, that it was my destiny and could not be shaken off. I felt that even if I had ten minutes on the Anfield pitch as a substitute and scored the winning goal it would all have been worth it.

There was one notable difference in this particular episode. On the night I'd smoked the cannabis I had watched a programme about Stephen Hawking and his theories on black holes. I soon became fixated on his revelations and theories. I began to believe I was in some way creating supermassive black holes in space with my brain and that they were going to destroy the world. The Liverpool delusion was stronger than the black holes delusion, but when the idea of causing the end of the world came it was very frightening and felt very real indeed. Five seconds would feel like five minutes as the pain drilled in and out of my brain. Time seemed to stand still and would then speed up. Emotions and senses would be monumentally magnified, bringing enormous joy one moment and then making my worst ever nightmare seem a reality. This was one of the scariest delusions I ever had. In a strange way, destroying the world through the creation of black holes actually seemed more plausible to me than doing so by having AIDS.

In the end I spent three months in a different hospital to the one I had worked at so I wouldn't bump into my workmates every day. When I was admitted the first thing I did was have a 'ciggie' in the smoke room. As I walked in, there on the floor in the middle of the room was a Liverpool leather football. As you might guess, I saw this as a sign. I believed it to mean that I wasn't deluded at all. Then, as I looked to my left, there was a lad sitting down who was obviously blind in one eye. He had the entire Liverpool home kit on, including the red shorts and socks.

I was so convinced I was going to play for Liverpool that by the end of my time on that ward, this lad too began to believe my story. It even got to the point that he bought the Bill Shankly biography and read it on the ward while he was still wearing his full Liverpool kit. My story of how Shankly had spoken to me in a vision had apparently made sense to him. He seemed to want my delusion to be true just as much as I did.

While I was there I felt that God was with me again. I would often ask to speak to the hospital chaplain and visit the chapel to pray, but it felt more like a cry for help than anything real. I didn't really know who God was. Something seemed to be blocking my connection to him. In fact, I still believed my delusion about playing for Liverpool was a mission from God. At times my experiences were so bad that the only answer was to go in search of God's grace. It seemed the only way out of the hell I found myself in.

During that admission I didn't sleep for nearly three weeks. I believed I would lose my dream of playing for

Liverpool if I did. I would force myself to stay awake night after night. Later, when I was recovering from the delusion, I was shocked by what a nurse told me: if I had been an older man, staying awake for three weeks could very easily have killed me. I was always aware of the possibility of death during my delusions but it never seemed a physical reality – not something that would happen to me. When I was discharged I vowed to myself to try and make this the last time I would end up in hospital. Enough was enough. I had to try harder.

CHAPTER NINE

The Key to Recovery

IN 2007 I MOVED OUT OF SUPPORTED living and into my own flat. It was an exciting time. I had now been well for two years and I was working at staying well. I was trying harder. Everyone thought I was ready for the change. I was apprehensive but excited at the same time. It was a real chance to get myself back in the game and make a new life for myself.

To recover I needed support from my family, especially my amazing parents. Thank God for Mum and Dad! I also needed to do a lot of work on my own recovery that I hadn't done before. After being discharged from the hospital in Chester I saw a psychologist every week for over five years. She was brilliant. She came to my supported living accommodation and then my new flat. At the beginning she allowed me to be angry and to express my bitterness and pain. Bit by bit, though, the cognitive behaviour therapy she was teaching me started to sink in. I gradually began to appreciate the fact that events affect our thoughts and emotions and then our actions. Even so, there were plenty of crisis points when I felt I couldn't go on and saw no hope. It was a slow and painful process.

My best friend Terry, whom I'd lived with at the supported living house, spent a lot of time at my flat. He was struggling with a mental health condition and an alcohol addiction. We were very close and saw each other most days. We'd watch art-house films, action films and dramas about people with real and often dark problems. We always found these characters strangely funny as we could identify with their problems.

Terry and I had been good friends for years and were almost like brothers; we had a very special bond. Humour wasn't far away as we shared a similar view on life. We tried to make the best of the bad situation we were both in and still have fun despite our problems. We'd go to Liverpool for nights out and helped each other through difficult times as well as good. We'd both been dealt similar cards in life and that drew us together. I had some of the best laughs I've ever had with him. One year we watched 'The Who' singing 'My Generation' at the Glastonbury Festival on television. We danced around the room bouncing off each other like we were sixteen years old, laughing our heads off.

As I had a spare room at my flat, Terry would often stay over. One morning, though, as we were watching television he had a huge fit right in front of me. He turned grey and I really thought he was going to die. I tried not to panic and rang the ambulance. It was one of the longest waits I ever had. When the ambulance came, thankfully he was okay, but it was a great shock to me. I realised for the first time that I had a responsibility of care when he stayed with me. It hadn't really dawned on me until then.

One day, Terry asked me whether I would still go out with a woman if she was older and had children. After thinking about it for a while I said that I would. He seemed surprised but as I was a bit older than him he managed to get his head around it. I was surprised too but even in the darkest nights of alcohol-fuelled escapism I had still looked forward to a time when things could get better for me. My support system of family, therapist and friends had given me a slender hope of brighter days to hold on to.

My mental health would disintegrate from time to time when I was in my flat. I would tend to panic thinking another serious episode was on the way. They were like little crisis points that I had to overcome but not give in to. Freedom was knocking. It was nearly time to let it in.

It was during one of these crises that God dramatically and finally broke into my life. (Some of you may be switching off now! Please bear with me because the transformation in my life as a result has been remarkable.) If what I'm about to tell you stirs up some questions in your heart about God then that is enough for me, and if it doesn't that's fine too.

It all happened on Easter Sunday, 2008. I had reached a crisis point and believed I would be on my way to hospital again. I had been in my new flat for about a year but I was soon experiencing the usual symptoms of a manic episode: sleepless nights, a loss of appetite, an increase in alcohol consumption and flights of fancy. All the usual alarm bells were ringing.

It had been three years since my last admission, which was the longest time I had ever stayed out of hospital since my illness had begun. I couldn't bear the idea of my life being ruined once more. I was desperate and in tears. After another sleepless night I decided to pray my heart out for help and for some peace from my troubling thoughts.

"Not again," I thought, "not after all the hard work I'd been doing with my therapist. Please, not again."

My prayers were immediately answered. It was as though a film was played in my head and Jesus was the director; he was showing me my options and guiding me through this very personal encounter.

First of all, I got a sense of what hell might be like for someone like me if I died right at that moment. I felt I would be in darkness alone, full of regret forever. I knew I'd wasted my life. I needed to change direction. I needed to save myself. I was being helped to realise just what was at stake.

I knew I needed to say sorry to God for wasting my life up to that point. I needed to take responsibility for my actions and stop blaming events from my past and other people's mistakes. I needed to ask for forgiveness and feel forgiven for the things I knew I'd done wrong in my life. For the first time in my life I was ready to ask.

I then felt Jesus was showing me my life in the future over a ten-year period with and without alcohol. I was made to think of the consequences of my actions when it came to drinking. He showed me that if I continued to drink alcohol I would be mentally ill again and again. I would probably have no family of my own and no wife or serious long-term relationship. I'd be in a living hell of regret, no doubt in pain and alone. It was a revelation I needed to receive. My eyes were being opened to what I needed to do and I had no hesitation at all but to respond. Without alcohol my illness would become more manageable. I was shown how not drinking would improve my chance of having a loving relationship and a better life. Not drinking would also give my medication better chance to work efficiently.

I felt better instantly. I saw a chink of light and walked towards it.

I was made to see how I needed to say sorry to my Maker for how I'd responded to the problems in my life. I'd often blamed God for the pain I'd suffered. I was ready to forgive God and ask him to forgive me. So I said sorry without question, not only to God but to all the people I was aware I'd hurt in my past. I asked Jesus to intercede for me and heal any wounds I may have caused.

Suddenly I sensed I should turn the radio on – something I normally never did. I felt guided to do it as part of what I was going through. Amazingly, the first words I heard when I switched the stereo to radio were "Jesus Christ".

I sat on the end of my bed and listened like I'd never listened to anything else before. The programme was about the Crucifixion and Resurrection of Jesus Christ. Until this I hadn't realised that it was Easter Sunday. I listened to every word, knowing without any doubt that what I was listening to was true. It had actually happened. Jesus had died for the world and he had died for me, to make me new, to make me free.

I knew what I needed to do. I must never get drunk again for the rest of my life. I felt that God had stepped into my life and intervened. I now realised what an influence my drinking had been on my mental health over the last twenty years and that stopping was the only way forward.

The result? Eight years have passed since then but I haven't been drunk since that day.

Looking back, I don't know why I didn't give up alcohol sooner. I can only assume that I wasn't ready or willing to let Jesus into my life. I didn't want to change. Maybe I felt that I didn't deserve my freedom, fooling myself into believing that I didn't even want it. In truth, my fears had been crippling me. I had held on to a past life in which alcohol had made me temporarily happy, not realising that day had long gone.

Not drinking alcohol has brought a sense of calm and order to my mind and my life. It is a constant reminder of the healing power of Jesus in my life. It is also a personal sign of my faith and proof to me that Jesus is alive today and can change broken lives. I thought not drinking would be hard but I have been able to accomplish it in God's strength. I found it easy to turn my back on something that I knew could make me really ill, yet it is God's strength that has enabled me to do so, not my own. Every time I've been in pubs or social events it has felt like there has been an invisible barrier between me and an alcoholic drink. I am so grateful to Jesus for this daily reminder of my faith.

And so on that day I became a Christian – an idea that was completely alien to me up to that point. I was not influenced by anyone in my understanding or making my decision, except perhaps for the experiences of God I had had earlier in life. I had simply reached the bottom of a pit with nowhere else to go but prayer. It was an instinct born out of complete brokenness that led me to being 'born again', a phrase meaning the new life that begins when you hand your life over to Jesus.

From that day forward my world has completely changed. I now view everything in a very different way. I have an inner peace that was lacking before. I also have hope for a better future which means I now enjoy an optimistic perspective of my life and the world I live in.

CHAPTER TEN

Spiritual Healing

BEFORE MY EASTER SUNDAY salvation, I was a shadow of my former self. At times I couldn't even leave my flat to buy milk as I was so scared I'd meet someone I knew. I was totally ashamed of who I was. I had no girlfriend and had not had a proper relationship for ten years. I had been unemployed for years and my spirit was broken with no hope for the future. Alcohol was my crutch and I was running away from all responsibility. I was haunted by a bad attitude. I had virtually given up on life but was trying to remain optimistic for my family and my therapist so as not to worry them.

Without Jesus I relied on people. My faith was in those who offered me help but they couldn't always be there and they couldn't live my life for me. With Jesus in my life I could for the very first time really start to make plans without the fear of being seriously mentally ill.

Eight years on, I am now a married man with two stepsons. I could never have believed that I could be a husband and a stepfather before my encounter with Jesus.

When I met the boys they were eleven and sixteen years old. Now they are eighteen and twenty-three, and growing into two lovely young men. It has been a total pleasure and privilege to be a small part of their lives and they have been so kind to me by letting me into their family. I know for sure that God has blessed us all as we have grown together through good and bad times.

One of the first books I read in my bible was Psalms and I remember in particular this scripture from Psalm 126: "Those who sow with tears will reap with songs of joy."[2] I can safely say that I am now indeed reaping that joy in my life. I pray that if bad times come I will remember that joy is often just around the corner.

After a year as a Christian I was baptised at my local Methodist church and made a speech to over a hundred people. If you would have asked me to do that a year before I would have run a mile. My entire family came to the baptism including my nephews and niece, which meant so much to me. New chapters of the story of my life were beginning to be written. I was truly beginning to leave my nightmare of a past behind.

After a year as a Christian I had another encounter with God. I read the book of Job from the Bible and I immediately related to it. It's a story about a man who loses everything and is totally broken by a pact between the Devil and God before being restored by God for his faith. I also listened to a sermon on Christian radio in which the preacher spoke about the book of Job and the importance of its message. I realized that everything that was happening to me was no coincidence or

---

[2] Psalm 126:5 (NIV)

just a crutch. I was being gradually healed by the power of the Father, the Holy Spirit and Jesus Christ. Like Job, I had been tested and would likely be tested again. I was slowly learning how having a faith would be so important in my new life, especially when it came to overcoming hardships or troubles.

My world had been flipped on its head and I felt I had thirty-six years of wrong thinking to flush down the drain. As I learnt and read more and more in the Bible, I found answers to why we suffer and why humanity has always got it wrong. I began to understand the way the world is and understood with sadness that people don't recognise or accept what Jesus has done for them.

I began to realize why we find it so hard to believe. All I needed to do was to ask why I didn't want to believe before I did. I clearly wasn't tuned in. I didn't understand or even comprehend who Jesus was and what he had done for me.

Thankfully I felt God's presence in my life was growing and felt like I belonged in his world again. That first year as a new Christian felt like another form of apprenticeship but an apprenticeship that finally mattered, that actually counted for something. For once I felt hopeful and excited about the future. The joy was amazing. I had been going around for so long in a haze, fighting disillusionment and illness, but now I was breaking free.

I was happy and in love after meeting my wife to be, Pam. We both enjoyed getting to know each other, and dating made me feel like a teenager again. I was really hopeful for our future together. It felt like our relationship was being blessed by God as she too shared my faith and we were so compatible. Love was being kind to me, probably for the first time in my life. My friend Terry must have been able to see into the future when he asked me if I would go out with a woman with children!

I could finally see the world of opportunity opening up in front of me. It was a revelation, like the delusions had felt in the past, but this time with my feet set firmly in reality. I was not deluded. God was real and was all around me. It was beautiful. I had a great desire to share what I was feeling with everyone I knew so they could share in the joy too. I felt like I had when God first came into my life but with a stronger hold and understanding of my faith and what God was capable of.

All of us go through periods of spiritual healing in our lives as we grow as people, although we might not necessarily identify our changing feelings as a spiritual process. Sometimes bitter lessons may be learnt through painful experiences and we don't associate that with God as we are taught that he is love. But, just like a strict parent, a period of spiritual healing is often a form of tough love. In this process we are defined as people and learn from our mistakes.

As I have recognized the journey I have been on, I have begun to greatly desire to help others see that spiritual healing is real. My recent experiences have shown me that all I needed to do in order to receive God's love was to truly believe I was forgiven, to let go and to let God in. Yet as I know only too well, believing is the hardest thing to do at times, especially when you have no real perception of what having a faith means.

Choosing faith in a psychiatrist and their prescription over real spiritual healing could be the reason so many people continue to suffer for so many years. I say this because that's what happened to me. I couldn't find it in me to believe in a God who was making my life so hard and painful.

My experience tells me that not believing is too easy. Taking the narrow road of faith in the unseen is much harder, especially as the modern world offers so many distractions. Staying as we are is safer. Change is often painful. To accept the existence of healings and miracles may challenge our belief system so much that we just tune out and potentially miss out on the blessing in the process.

Before I was touched by spiritual healing I found myself in a very dark place with no hope and no future. The majority of people will fortunately never find themselves in a place like that and might therefore think spiritual healing is not for them. But we all need to be touched by the mystical healing power of God. A person's spirit can be broken by life; one may be in desperate need of being blessed but not know where to turn to for help.

Faith is a key component in healing. To trust in God with all our heart is the hardest thing to do at times but people who have come to faith know without doubt that they've had a personal encounter with God.

Finally, I believe there doesn't have to be a crisis point before we ask for our spirits to be healed. We may see God working his miracles in someone else or just know we've been experiencing something special in our own lives for some time. We may know instinctively that we need to move in a different direction. We may feel guided to act in a certain way that means we need to change how we live. As I know only too well, many of us don't feel ready to make that change and so we stay as we are.

Understanding what Jesus did for us on the cross is the most crucial factor in our healing. It is this that made me stop and change direction. When he walked on the earth, Jesus was a healer. When he died and was resurrected that healing became available to the world, to everyone, to you and to me. All we need to do is ask for it and wait.

I would like to be able to say that I lived happily ever after with no more struggles. But life, even the life of a Christian, is not like that while we are still here on earth. When we give our lives to Jesus, there is sometimes a dramatic change, such as the freedom from alcohol addiction that I experienced. But there are other things that take time to heal, and we learn more about God, about ourselves and about others on the journey. For me, the risk of manic episodes still remains and on occasion I have fallen back into delusions. Yet God is still faithfully working on me and gradually healing me. The Bible describes this as being changed "from glory to glory"[3].

Why not begin your journey today?

---

[3] 2 Corinthians 3:8 (KJV)

Afterword

THERE ARE PEOPLE WITH WORSE mental health conditions than mine. I have met some of them. I see the mentally ill as some of the bravest people on the planet. Tremendous amounts of courage are needed to endure our illnesses and then to recover over and over again. This is something that is overlooked by society as a whole and, sadly, even by some mental health employees; people are naturally afraid of things they don't understand. Unless you've lost your own mind you can never really relate to someone who has. But more people must try to have sympathy and respect for those who have.

We hear too much negative publicity about mental health incidents in our national media, which only adds to the mass hysteria and stigma. In my opinion we should be flooding the media with positive stories of recovery, dispelling some of the myths that have been created over the years. Mentally ill people are not all dangerous and violent. They are often just oversensitive members of society who are too ashamed to admit their conditions publicly out of fear of ridicule and shame.

Successive governments are failing the mentally ill by not providing sufficient funds or facilities. Instead, we have seen more cuts in mental health services than anywhere else in the NHS. This is not only dangerous but also irresponsible. It sums up the general lack of understanding for people who need enormous amounts of help.

Things may be about to change, though, as mental health is now being talked about more. I hope this will continue and that changes will take place that improve the care for the most vulnerable people in our society.

Matthew Siddle
2016

What Shall I Read Next?

Publisher's Recommendation

Northern Soul
David O'Brien
ISBN 978-1-910197-59-2

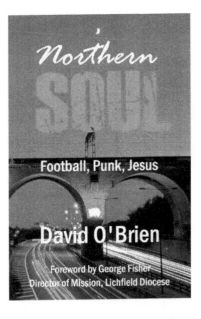

Would it bother you if your vicar or pastor was a former skinhead, punk-rocker and football hooligan? What about your Sunday School teacher?

This is a timely modern story of how God chooses sinners, any of us, and makes them into saints for his glory. David O'Brien was a least likely candidate for church leadership but God had his eye on him from his childhood amidst the ordinary working class culture of Greater Manchester.

Available from all good bookshops or from the publisher:

www.onwardsandupwards.org/product/northern-soul

22899245R00051

Printed in Great Britain
by Amazon